Lived Experience and Comparison
Of Five Views of the Human

Bernard J. Fleury, Ed.D.

Lived Experience and Comparison   Bernard J. Fleury Ed.D.

Kurt E. Miller, Technology Consultant.

Printed by Create Space, an Amazon.com Company.

ISBN-13: 978-1544762234

ISBN-10: 1544762232

Website: www.intolifebylight.com

Printed in the United States of America

Table of Contents

Author Biography: Meet Bernard Video and Narrative. www.intolifebylight.com/about/author

LinkedIn Profile: www.linkedin.com/in/bernard-fleury-a4411541

Description

Article 1:

Know that evolution is a purpose driven process with the human phenomenon with its unique reflective human consciousness is at its very core.

What if evolution is the ascent to consciousness, with man, the human, with the most highly developed consciousness as the leading shoot of evolution?

Article 2:

Know that man, an existent who is most human when engaging in the I-Thou relationship with his creator and fellow persons.

What if for married persons, the principle I-Thou relationship should be with each other?

What if the principle I-Thou relationship for each person is with God-a relationship mirrored in the I-Thou relationship of married persons?

Article 3:

Know that man, is simply a collection of innate impulses to act.

What if "learned to do by doing" is the way to develop our children's "innate impulses to act" from being random and inchoate, to having a definite structure through interaction with a carefully planned classroom environment?

Article 4:

Know that man, the primary existent, who determines his own essence by the choices he makes. He is a god unto himself.

What if I, a unique individual self, am the basic reality, the "prime existent"?

What if I possess internal freedom-am not determined (programmed) but can be *influenced* by my environment *if I choose to be*?

What if there is no predefined human nature, no single concept of man because there is no God to define man and "nothing", my origin, doesn't define me?

What if the basis of choose is my own freedom?

What if I, a man, am "condemned to be free"-even though I did not create myself, I am responsible for all that follows once I exist?

What if whether or not God exists is irrelevant because even if He does exist He would play a part in my life only if I choose to believe in Him, and choose to let Him play a part in my life?

What if life is absurd because there is no empirical justification for man's existence, no "reason" for living, except the reasons each man chooses for his own life?

Article 5:

Know that man is a reactive organism whose behavior is shaped and maintained by the consequences of a selective environment.

What if man the human was and is nothing more than a purely natural creature like the rat and pigeon except that man has a much more highly complex brain and nervous system?

Article 6:

Know that Buber's and de Chardin's views of man, the human, are the two theistic views among the five views of man I present in my revised book in answer to the question what is man?

What if both Buber and de Chardin believe that the Other-Than-Us a transcendent god, is the starting point in their view of man, the human?

What if de Chardin and Buber believe that man, the human is a person, and that Person is at the heart of the universe because the Other-Than-Us, god, is a person (three persons for de Chardin)?

What if de Chardin and Buber would agree that their theory (view) of man is based on the synthesis of philosophy, science, and religion?

Article 7:

Know that John Dewey's view of man is one of the atheistic view of the three atheistic views (J.P. Sartre and B.F. Skinner) of man that I present in my revised book in answer to the question *what is man.*

What if Dewey believes that "in truth experience knows no division between human concerns and a purely mechanical physical world. Man's home is nature: his purposes and aim are dependent for execution upon natural conditions"?

What if Buber and de Chardin absolutely disagree with Dewey? They believe that man is a body-mind-spirit complex made in the image and likeness of God and destined for final union with Him.

Article 8:

Know that Sartre, Buber, and de Chardin agree that I (each man) am a unique individual self.

What if according to Buber and de Chardin, I am not the basic reality, the prime existent?

What if according to Buber and de Chardin, "nothing" is not my origin? My parent and God are my origin.

What if I possess internal freedom am not determined or programmed but prior to the age of reason my environment can imprint me for life?

What if there is a definite human nature predefined by God and the children's parents?

What if the basis for choose is my own freedom but my choose needs to be based on an "informed conscious"?

What if de Chardin, Sartre, and Buber agree that we are "free" whether we like it or not?

Article 9:

Know that Skinner believed the basic substance of the universe is physical matter, which takes many forms.

What if Buber and de Chardin would absolutely disagree?

What if Skinner defines man as a biological organism who needs to be studied through a science of human behavior so that the behavior of man can be controlled and the human condition improved?

What if Buber and de Chardins' views are compatible with man being a biological organism in part but that is only the "without" of him and omits the "within" which is the source of all the components that Skinner lists under autonomous man?

Purpose Statement

I wrote this e-Book to describe my actual lived experience of the five philosophers' views in my own life and career as a teacher, principal, and college professor.

How much these views affect each person who reads this e-Book will differ accordingly to the person's personality and career.

Introduction

This Mini E-Book is intended to be a companion book to my Self-Understanding Guidebook,

What is Man?
Male and Female

published 11/11/2011 and to be launched on February 15, 2012. This Mini E-Book's contents provide the Author's many years of lived experience researching and teaching their views to university students preparing for careers as school personnel.

The "Comparison" articles will give the reader basic information regarding the theistic and atheistic views of what it means to be human – where the two groups agree and where they disagree.

It is my hope to bring to my readers a deeper understanding of who they are as humans and of their own lived human experience.

Article 1

My Lived Experience of Pierre Teilhard de Chardin's
View of What it Means to be Human

My lived experience of Teilhard de Chardin's view of What is Man? What does it mean to be human? began in 1962 when one of my teachers in the school where I was the principal gave me a copy of Teilhard's book <u>The Phenomenon of Man</u> (first published in English in 1958). I had been introduced to the theory of Darwinian Evolution and man's place in it in 1950 in my biology classes in Seminary.

But Teilhard de Chardin was the priest-scientist who proposed that Evolution has a direction – change and process are directed. Evolution is a purpose driven process with the human phenomenon with its unique reflective consciousness at its very core. De Chardin describes evolution as the ascent to consciousness, with man, the human as the most highly developed consciousness, as the leading shoot of evolution, the arrow pointing the way for further evolutionary development toward Omega Point: a final fulfillment of the world through a creative union with Omega (God).

I literally devoured Teilhard's view on man.

Why?

For a number of reasons:

When I first learned about his views in 1962 I had already come to believe in a Christianity which encompassed faith and reason – as essential elements. I developed this belief during the first two years of Seminary where our "religion" class was called "Apologetics" the defense or proof of Christianity based on reason and faith (biblical revelation and tradition).

That belief grew stronger when I came to know Teilhard's view of man beginning in 1962. Teilhard's view of man as the leading shoot of evolution is based on his scientific view that the process of evolution can be basically described as an ascent to consciousness from the very beginning, in a personalizing universe. The universe is "personalizing" because its origin (Alpha) (God) is a Person (three Persons in Christianity) but a single Being. As I wrote earlier, evolution to Teilhard has a direction, and that direction is marked by an ever increasing consciousness in man that culminates in Omega Point – final union with Omega (God).

Faith and reason complement each other although each has its own domain and way to knowledge. Faith is an action of our "within" – our freely choosing to believe someone or something which cannot be proven by logic or scientific method – someone like Jesus Christ and something like the Bible or Tradition. Reason involves logic, using a form of valid inference. Scientific method involves logical reasoning using a set procedure to arrive at a conclusion in the empirical (physical) realm.

Faith and Reason combined teach us that Mind-Body-Spirit are intimately related and interdependent. The Complex of these three forms the human being.

The human is first of all a person, not a thing – unique in the biosphere, the sphere of life. I, a human am the only creature who is a person, a being created by God at the moment God directly infuses the soul into the tiny fertilized egg – the moment of conception. My body evolves like other living bodies. But in the case of human evolution is focused on the complexification of the brain and nervous system so that the "within" of man could express itself in our earth lives.

God made man in His own Image – Male and Female He created them. (Genesis)

The Term "Man" (human) applies to Male and Female although sexually "Man" equals male, and "Woman" equals female.

God, the Alpha, the beginner of life, creates each person as unique with a specific plan for his or her life unlike any other human's life. God doesn't make junk, so each person's life is of infinite value. The overall ascent of consciousness is affected positively or negatively, even if only in a small way, by how we choose to live our lives.

We image God by being a person as He is (Three Persons) but so united as to equal One God, able to love another person and give ourselves completely to that person through the bodily expression of that love given and shared between two persons in the committed relationship of marriage. The complete self-giving of each person to the other person mirrors the relationship between the persons of the Trinity – a love relationship that is so profound that the three persons constitute but one Divine Being, One God.

Like Teilhard, I believe that Man was created by God for his (man's) own sake – destined for Omega Point – a final union with Omega, God, Who is our first beginning and our last end – the Alpha and Omega of our lives.

Article 2

My Lived Experience of Martin Buber's
View of What it Means to be Human

My lived experience of Martin Buber's View of what it means to be human is of dialogue – relationship – meeting. My principal I-Thou dialogue relationship in terms of frequency and duration, is with God, The Other-Than-Us primarily in the person of Jesus Christ, my Lord with a human face, who knows what it is like to walk this earth as a man. He reaches out to me just as I am and I respond with, "Jesus, I trust in You."

On a completely human love relationship basis, my principal I-Thou relationship is with my wife. I had briefer glimpses (in terms of frequency and duration) of I-Thou dialogue relationships with two of my brother Deacons: John O'Brien, especially during my wife's and my four day visit with him in 2009, and with Thomas Callahan on a number of occasions during our ministry.

A much longer (like sixty-five years) I-Thou dialogue relationship has been and continues to be a joyful experience with my friend and spiritual counselor Father Vincent O'Connor.

All real living is meeting – my prayer life is repeated meetings several times each day for praying the Liturgy of the Hours, the Rosary, and The Chaplet of Divine Mercy. There are also spontaneous prayers in between regular prayer times, especially in crises but also just in everyday living events when I look to Him for wisdom – I ask and then I truly listen. He speaks back sometimes through direct thoughts and often through others, especially my wife, and through unforeseen events in my life.

I believe I also had some brief I-Thou dialogue relationships with my Junior, Senior, and Graduate School college students especially during advisement sessions each semester.

My lived experiences of dialogue-relationship meeting, convince me that I have lived Buber's key concepts. All real living is meeting and all truly human meeting takes place within the I-Thou dialogue relationship.

I also believe with Buber that Man as a species is unique from all other species and each human person within the species is unique from every other person.

My primary attribute as a human is that I am a person, a subject rather than an object. I am made in the image of the Supreme Person, the Other-Than-Us, God the Father. As a man, a human person, I am a body-spirit complex existing in both time and eternity. I participate in finitude by

9

the fact that my knowledge is finite (limited). I participate in infinity by the fact that I know at all; that is, that I have the capacity for immediate awareness (intuition) and for reflective thought.

As Buber taught and I agree, as a man, I am the only creature of which we are presently aware, who knows his entire life that he must die and to a certain extent I control my dying by the choices I make. I can commit willful suicide or hasten the end of my earth life by simply not taking proper care of myself.

My human freedom and choice are another of my unique qualities and capacities as a person. As Buber taught, my actions are unforeseeable and really unpredictable in both their nature and extent. The fact that I am as a man, a human person, both a reasoning, and a feeling being, contributes to the basic unpredictability of my actions. Both reason and feeling are distinctive human attributes, both are important. But feeling, valuing, responding, make reasoning personal, make reasoning an effective part of each person's repertoire, each person's response to life. Since according to Buber, all real living is meeting, and at least one party in meeting must be a human person, I am most human when I engage in an I-Thou dialogue relationship.

But, there is a distinct place for the I-It, the subject-object relationship. It is the proper relationship when one is engaged in scientific method, in evaluation of the results of an experiment or in correcting Objective Tests. I-It is an essential part of living and working.

Summary: My lived experiences of dialogue-relationship-meeting, convince me that I have lived all three concepts. All real living is meeting and all truly human meeting takes place within the I-Thou dialogue relationship.

Article 3

My Lived Experience of John Dewey's View of

What it Means to be Human

Part One: My Preparation

As a History major working toward teacher certification in the early 1950's, I was soon introduced to the views of John Dewey, particularly in "Methods of Teaching" class. It involved preparation of Units and Lesson Plans that stressed the active participation of children in real life projects, like studying the life of a plant by growing one from seed, caring for it, keeping a chart of its growth, etc. "Learn to do by doing" was the way to develop our children's "innate impulses to act" from being random and inchoate, to having a definite structure through interaction with the carefully planned classroom environment. This environment would shape these impulsive tendencies into habits that would make our students socially efficient – able to live productive lives in the particular society in which they were growing up.

My training as a public school teacher was far different than what I had experienced for my elementary, high school, and first two years as a student in a "Junior College", all three of which were Catholic Institutions, the first two taught by sisters and the college years by priests.

My view of man when I began my public college education as a junior at our State University was that "Man is a creature composed of body and soul, and made in the image and likeness of God".

There was a definite hierarchy of knowledge with Knowledge of God as defined by our faith was first, the Mathematics, Science, Languages (English Language and Literature, Latin, and French), were the curriculum in High School.

These subjects were prepared for in eight years of Elementary School – no Kindergarten – by Catechism Classes, Reading, Writing (Grammar and Composition), Arithmetic (Addition, Subtraction, Multiplication and Division), with Algebra (beginning in Grade Eight), History (U.S.) and World (Ancient, Medieval, and Modern), General Science, Music, Art, and Penmanship.

Except for Religious classes, brief prayers every hour, and some worship services at the Church, my Curriculum for the first twelve years was nearly identical to what was taught in the public schools where daily reading of a portion of the Bible without written notes or oral comment, and the singing of a song (often a hymn or Carol at Christmas time), were common practice.

Only "progressive" public schools and the public schools in my town were not "progressive" stressed "learn to do by doing."

I had great difficulty reconciling my view of man as the catechism defined him with Dewey's view of man as a purely natural creature – no soul or spirit – just a collection of innate impulses to act. But, I had no problem with Dewey's "Learn to do by doing" because that was my own personal "best way" to learn.

I finished all my education classes for the Master's Degree in Education during my first year and three months as a teaching Principal in 1954-1955. All I needed was to write my dissertation. To reconcile my own conflicts regarding Dewey's view of man and what I had been taught, I chose as my dissertation topic: A Comparative Study of the Philosophies of Education of John Dewey and Jacques Maritain. Maritain was a Catholic Scholastic Philosopher whose teachings on man were the underpinnings of Catholic parochial education at the time.

My Advisor at the University was the Dean of Education who really understood John Dewey but nothing about Jacques Maritain. So I had to get a second advisor, the President of Elms College our local Catholic College for women! That fact alone shows the major and wide division between Dewey's view of Man and the traditional Christian view.

Article 3

My Lived Experience of John Dewey's View of

What it Means to be Human

Part Two: My Teaching Career

From the time I began my career in public school education in April 1954 as a Teaching Principal, I was very Deweyan in my classroom environment and methods of teaching. My classroom was filled with various plants that had a tie in with our curriculum. We had coffee, banana, and citrus trees (dwarf), an aquarium with tropical fish, and at intervals various birds, turtles, guinea pigs, etc. The trees were living examples of major products grown in the countries we were studying in Grade Six. We had text books but children chose topics out of them to do their own project and I set up Learning Centers that had projects within them that the children could develop or choose their own. We had Social Studies and Science Fairs where pupils from each grade in the school could design and set up their individual projects. A rating card developed jointly by teachers and students evaluated each student's presentation and project. Prizes were awarded on a number of points earned basis – so theoretically everyone could get first prize if their point score was high enough. Parents were active participants both in helping their children and in attending the public Fairs held in the Town Hall.

But I also believed that each of my students was a child of God and heir of Heaven – made in God's image and likeness. They had a free will and could choose how they would relate to each other and to the teacher. Together we developed a list of classroom behaviors and posted a Self-Discipline Chart with each child's name on it next to the posted list of behaviors. For consistently violating one of those behaviors over the school day a checkmark was placed at end of the day beside the child's name. Penalties were attached to each additional checkmark leading to a conference with parents and terminating with "unsatisfactory conduct" checked on the Report Card at Report Card Time (four times a year).

On the positive side, consistent keeping of the behaviors listed over a two day period led to the erasure of one checkmark. It was a highly effective system after it was in effect for a month or so. As the Principal I was often called out of my class to deal with some pressing issue. The teacher who covered for me by leaving the door between her room and mine opened often told me that my children behaved better when I was out of the room than when I was there! Allowances that the total class understood were "special" for any special needs children we had.

I carried my Deweyan teaching methods into my College career in 1968 when I became an Assistant Professor at what is now Westfield State University. With the help of a grant from the Kettering Foundation Education Branch, The Institute for the Development of Educational Activities, a colleague and myself organized a Learning Community that Education Majors could opt into. They had three ways to "take" our courses. The first was the conventional way: Lecture, Textbook Reading and Discussion, and Written Tests. The second was through Learning Centers developed by the professors with student input that were set up in three classrooms. The third way was to do a self-chosen project to meet the objectives of each course with an initial conference with a professor and "progress" conferences at stated intervals, culminating in a presentation to others who had chosen the same option. Evaluation was based on a "score" card developed by a joint professor – student team. The project student and professor using the score card each evaluated the project. They then met to discuss their evaluations and assign a score that translated into a letter grade for the course.

I was Deweyan in my academic teaching methods and Christian in my beliefs and character formation methods of what is man? What does it mean to be human? As Joseph Culliton wrote in his classic book, <u>A Processive World View For Pragmatic Christians</u> (1975),
….most naturalistic and pragmatic insights and values are not opposed to Christian thought….that faith in a transcendent God is made more vital when it is enriched and supported by a natural faith in man and the universe…when naturalistic, pragmatic thought is reincorporated within Christian thought, both are revitalized and enriched, (Book Jacket).

Article 4

My Lived Experience of Jean-Paul Sartre's View of

What it Means to be Human

My lived experience of Jean-Paul Sartre's view of man – what it means to be human, is based on over forty years of study, pondering, and teaching on the following seven "Essential Points" on What is Man? that Sartre proposes:

1. I, a unique, individual self, am the basic reality, the "prime existent".
   Since God does not exist, there is at least one being (man) in whom existence precedes essence. Man exists, turns up, appears on the scene. At first I am nothing because nothing is my origin.
2. But I possess internal freedom – am not determined (programmed), but can be <u>influenced</u> by my environment <u>if</u> I <u>choose</u> to be.
3. There is no predefined human nature, no single concept of "man" because there is no God to define man and "nothing", my origin, doesn't define me.
   So, each man defines himself by the choices he makes which begins when a person is mature enough to make choices and doesn't end until the individual person's death. So, as long as there are living persons, the definition of "man" is open and changing.
4. The basis for choice is my own freedom. Man is his own plan of action. I am most a man when I make "authentic" choices, that is, choices which take into consideration the fact that "no man is an island unto himself" – what I do affects others – the effect of my choice on others must be taken into account by <u>me</u>.
5. I , man, am "condemned to be free" – even though I did not create myself, I am responsible for all that follows once I exist. I am my own plan of action. To be <u>free</u> does not mean that I obtain what I wish for. It is rather the choice by which I decide to wish. Success in getting what I wish for is <u>not</u> important to freedom. <u>Freedom is the ultimate reality</u> – a value in itself. (Bernard J. Fleury, <u>What is Man?</u> pp. 193-194)

With regard to essential point number one, my lived experience tells me that I am <u>not</u> the prime existent nor is my origin "nothing".

God is the Prime Existent. He is my origin, my beginning, and my last end. I recognize Sartre's dilemma. He acknowledges that there are two possible answers to man's origin God and nothing, and he chooses nothing. After more than forty years of study and pondering it makes far more sense to me that Someone created me out of nothing – that's what the word "create" means with reference to God. How God created me, and all that exists, is not the principal question.

I believe essential point number two. All human persons possess free will and we do determine what we become as a person over a lifetime of choices. These choices are <u>influenced</u> by many factors such as our genetic makeup, our parents who are or first teachers, educators, clergy, siblings, friends, and yes our enemies!

Because humans were and are created by God, man has a defined nature. He is a mind-body-spirit being, a person, created for his own sake with a specific divinely given plan for his life. Man's body came through an act of human love by his parents. His soul was directly willed by God at each person's bodily conception. No two of us are <u>exactly</u> alike.

However we can thwart God's specific plan for each of our lives by using our free will to make choices that are self-destructive – not being open to God's grace and prompting in our decision making.

I agree with essential point number five. We are "condemned to be free". I did not ask to be conceived or born but I am, once I reach the age of reason and have no major mental disability, responsible for choices I make, and I must make choices to live. In any given instance, <u>not</u> making a choice <u>is</u> a choice!

Essential point number six is true in the sense that the part that God plays in each human life is affected by whether we believe that God exists, and then choose to let Him play a part in our decision making. But, that presumes that our God is passive without our choosing to believe in Him. The Bible is filled with stories of God's direct intervention in human affairs like the Burning Bush which set Moses' ministry in motion and the Annunciation which resulted in Jesus' incarnation. As essential point number seven says: "Life is absurd" if we believe that there is no empirical justification for man's existence, no "reason" for living, except the reasons each man chooses for his own life.

My comments on points number three and five indicate that there is a justification for my existence and how I am supposed to live my life. My life is absurd if do not believe that I am on this earth for a Divinely willed reason.

If you want to deepen your self-knowledge of how atheistic existentialism has profoundly affected your own self-image and the culture around you, read my new book <u>What is Man? Male and Female</u> , Part Four, pages 157-196 and my Mini E-Book, <u>Lived Experience and Comparison of Five Views of the Human </u>both of which will be available on Amazon.com beginning on Launch Day, February 15, 2012.

Article 5

My Lived Experience of B.F. Skinner's View of

What is Man? What does it Mean to be Human?

B.F. Skinner's experiments from which came his theory of Behavior Modification were done with rats and pigeons. His observations involved his now famous invention the "Skinner Box" – a sound-proof enclosure. Inside were buttons and levers that animals press to receive food pellets for doing whatever the experimenter wanted them to do.

Skinner preferred to call his invention an "Operant Conditioning Apparatus". It was a crucial tool for demonstrating his notion that rewarded behavior is repeated.

I saw film presentations of both the rat and pigeon experiments in my Methods of Teaching classes at the University. I also saw and was appalled by film presentations of newborn babies being placed face down for brief periods of time in tubs of warm water to observe their "innate" swimming movements and pricking them with small pins in their arms to observe their reflexes to pain. I couldn't control myself from blurting aloud: "I would never permit these experiments with any child of mine!" The experiments were not done by Skinner himself but by other Psychiatrists who were Skinnerian Behaviorists.

Skinner generalized from conditioned rat and pigeon behavior to operant conditioning methods for human persons.

To Skinner, man, the human, was and is nothing more than a purely natural creature like the rat and pigeon except that man has a much more highly complex brain and nervous system.

I observed operant conditioning in action in a number of Special Needs classrooms where I was supervising Student Teachers. I also experienced being part of a team to help develop Individualized Educational Plans (IEP's), based on formal testing and observations of children with specific disabilities that affected their Academic (cognitive) and Behavioral (affective) performance. These Individualized plans were then supposed to be the Guide for educating the particular child for whom they were designed. This was not always the case especially when the IEP was particularly demanding of the teacher in terms of the amount of individual time involved, especially if the teacher did not have an aide.

The same would be true for parents with a special needs child whose IEP demanded "all waking time" behavior modification. Parents are usually part of the IEP planning team and must have the time, skill, and self-sacrificing dedication to give their child what the Plan demands.

The classroom and the home environment also must be structured in such a way that only desired behavior is rewarded. Children (and persons of any age) must be exposed to carefully planned stimuli at regular intervals until the desired behavior is habitual.

Then a schedule of reinforcement must also be in place with stated intervals to expose the person to the effective stimuli so that the desired behavior remains habitual.

Behavior Modification that lasts is not a one shot deal. It remains a continuous process, sometimes for life!

I have also experienced through telephone calls, letters, and students who visited there, the lifestyle of the Walden II, Twin Oaks Community in Louisa, Virginia. The concept for the Commune was developed by Skinner in his 1948 book, Walden II, which described Skinner's ideal of how his Operant Conditioning would shape Skinnersville. To my knowledge, Skinner was unique among utopian writers in that he first described what it would be like to live out his Operant Conditioning Lifestyle and then some twenty-three years later describes his theoretical framework for Walden II in Beyond Freedom and Dignity in 1971.

Twin Oaks still exists in 2011. Just enter "Twin Oaks Community" on the web and note how the community has developed in its journey to live out B.F. Skinner's principles since its founding in 1967.

Article 6

Martin Buber's and Teilhard de Chardin's

Views of Man Compared

Buber's and de Chardin's views of man, the human, are the two theistic views among the five views of man I present in my new book in answer to the question, What is Man?

Buber believes in the primacy of person because the Other-Than-Us (God) is the Supreme, the first Thou with whom man has a personal I-Thou Dialogue relationship. The more the contact with the Thou, the fuller is the sharing, the meeting.

His view is also social and experiential. True community is present when each individual accepts full responsibility for the other. I am my brother's keeper! A lived life, concrete real experience, makes life experiential.

Lastly, there is an actional quality about man and human living. We can't go back because yesterday is history. We must go through if we know where we want of go from the present, the now. Our future in each age is a continuation of what went before, what we have actually experienced. It can also be a refutation of all or part of our past as we think about where we have been.

Teilhard de Chardin asserts that Man, the most highly developed consciousness is the leading shoot of evolution, the arrow pointing the way for further evolutionary development toward Omega Point, a final fulfillment of the world through creative union with Omega.

Teilhard asserts that Purpose Driven Evolution is the way the entire universe developed.

His view of Man, the Human, is based on a synthesis of philosophy, science, and religion.

Psychic energy (Light) centered in One Being, God, who is a Trinity of Three Divine Persons, is the active source for the beginning of the Evolutionary Process which can be described as the ascent to increased consciousness in terms of awareness, personalization, and reflective thought.

So, consciousness and person are at the heart of the universe which is a personalizing universe. Purpose Driven Evolution has a goal or Point: a final fulfillment of the world through creative union with Omega – with God.

Buber and de Chardin Compared

Both Buber and de Chardin believe that the Other-Than-Us, a transcendent God is the starting point in their view of Man, the human. They also believe that man, the human, is a person and that Person is at the heart of the universe because the Other-Than Us, God is a person (three Persons for Teilhard). Both also see God as One Divine Being, The Thou. Buber doesn't focus on Evolution as de Chardin does but I am confident, after forty years of research, that deChardin would agree with Buber that the I-Thou dialogue relationship with God is the primary relationship that makes a man most human. It is meant to be part of man's everyday life – his reason for being.

Teilhard and Buber would agree that their theory (view) of man is based on a synthesis of philosophy, science, and religion. Buber focuses on his view of philosophical anthropology. But he also asserted that the introspective, historical, and ontological (the branch of metaphysics which studies the nature of existence or being) are to be added to the functional and experimental as equals, for in the study of man they are ultimately superior.

Teilhard focuses on man as the leading shoot of evolution because among the primates he has the most highly developed "within". His a Mind-Body-Spirit complex being who will reach his goal of final union with Omega, God, as part of the entire human community which is united as one in its focus on Jesus Christ as the love object that draws all humankind together.

The only place where I believe that Buber and de Chardin would disagree would be who Jesus Christ was and is to Teilhard and all Christians: the Son of God, the Messiah, the Savior of the entire human species, and the love object who will draw all men together.

Article 7

Martin Buber's and Teilhard de Chardin's
Views of Man Compared to John Dewey's

John Dewey's view of man is one of the Atheistic views of the three Atheistic views of man that I present in my new book in answer to the question, What is Man?

This is the first and major point of contrast with the theistic views of Martin Buber and Teilhard de Chardin.

To Dewey, Man is a purely natural creature – a collection of random and inchoate innate impulses to act – shaped by interaction with a social medium – parent, teacher, environment.

In his book Democracy and Education (p. 333) Dewey writes "In truth experience knows no division between human concerns and a purely mechanical physical world. Man's home is nature; his purposes and aim are dependent for execution upon natural conditions. Separated from such conditions they become empty dreams and idle indulgences of fancy"....

Dewey's insistence on man as continuous and one with nature leads him to reject the idea of a separate and spiritual soul, mind, or consciousness in man, as this idea would destroy the unity of man with material nature and this unity seems all important to Dewey.

Dewey's denial of the soul as a separate spiritual principle leads him to deny the existence of consciousness and mind, taken in the sense of a self or consciousness exercising an influence on some object, as if the self or consciousness were itself outside the real object. As J. Brown writes in Educational Implications of Four Conceptions of Human Nature (p. 5) "The point is that a 'separate knower', separate, that is, from the thing known, cannot be tolerated." The direct implications of the denial of a separate knower distinct from the thing known is that it denies once and for all the existence of anything objective like truth, being, goodness, or God, and makes everything subjective and dependent on a mind that is inextricably entwined with and part of nature. All traditional concepts that regard man as a creature composed of body and soul, of a material and a spiritual principle, a "without" and a "within" are therefore false and unscientific according to Dewey.

Both Buber and de Chardin would absolutely disagree with Dewey here. Man is a body-mind-spirit complex, made in the image and likeness of God and destined for final union with Him.

Dewey maintains that there is no hierarchy of knowledge – no one subject worth anymore than any other. The criteria for choosing any subject are child interest and social efficiency. Thus

Dewey would advocate teaching the four R's, reading, writing, and arithmetic, and today he would probably add computer literacy. These skill subjects help children become socially efficient, able to express their interests in speaking, writing, and on the internet. But even here, the topics used to teach the four R's would still be based on child interest.

Both Buber and de Chardin have a distinct hierarchy of knowledge in both the cognitive and the affective domains that make it possible for a person to know the "real world", both the "within" (affective – domain of valuing) and the "without" (the cognitive – mathematics, sciences). They take for granted that the Four R's (add computer literacy) are necessary to master the Liberal Arts and Sciences.

According to Dewey, Social Efficiency – a socially useful life is the human's destiny. But Dewey writes of Social Efficiency as the goal of education only in the sense that Social Efficiency is an essential quality of education and not in the sense of Social Efficiency as an absolute goal. There is no absolute role or goal of education to act as a guide for planning, only the concept of Social Efficiency as a constantly changing norm by which a constantly changing education will shape itself.

Change that is constant and ongoing seems to be Dewey's ultimate – a very difficult concept to grasp. How can constant change be man's end or goal? Some fifty years after doing my Master's dissertation on A Comparative Study of the Philosophies of Education of John Dewey and Jacques Maritain and reading all of Dewey's Books, I still do not understand how the concept of constant change can be man's goal or end.

Buber and de Chardin pose a definite goal or end for each human person: final union with the Other-Than-Us, Omega, God! I understand and accept this view as man's destiny.

Article 8

Martin Buber's and Teilhard de Chardin's

Views of Man Compared to Jean-Paul Sartre's

Jean-Paul Sartre's view of man is another of the atheistic views of the three such views of man that I present in my new book in answer to the question, What is Man?

We will compare Buber's and de Chardin's views of man utilizing five of Sartre's major points he uses to present his concept of man, the human.

1. I, a unique, individual self, am the basic reality, the "prime existent". Since God does not exist, there is at least one being (man) in whom existence precedes essence. Man exists turns up; appears on the scene. At first I am nothing because NOTHING is my origin. Buber and de Chardin would agree that each human person is a unique, individual self. They would not agree that Man is the basic reality or the Prime Existent. The Other-Than-Us, God, is the Prime Existent who brings each man into being by infusing into each fertilized egg produced by the sexual union of a man and woman, an immortal soul – and another human person begins life in his or her mother's womb. So God rather than NOTHING is the origin of each person.

2. But I possess internal freedom – am not determined or programmed, but can be influenced by my environment if I choose to be.
   Buber and de Chardin would agree with Sartre that each human person has a free will, internal freedom, the capacity to make free choices. But, prior to the age of reason at least, my environment can not only influence what I become but even imprint me for life. Things like child abuse whether physical or emotional shape a child internally and externally. Basically, Buber and deChardin would agree that after the age of reason dawns in a specific child – the actual year of the age of reason varies with each child – that the "normal" child can make free choices influenced but not determined by his or her environment.

3. There is no predefined human nature, no single concept of "Man" because there is no God to define Man and "NOTHING", my origin, doesn't define me. So, each person defines himself by the choices he makes which begin when a person is mature enough to make choices and doesn't end until the individual person's death. So, as long as there are living persons, the definition of "Man" is open and changing.
   Buber and deChardin assert that there is a definite human nature predefined by God who created him. But they would agree with Sartre that the choices each person makes during his or her lifetime do define who that person becomes and most important of all, the

25

individual's pattern of choices either lead him or her to the person's intended union with God or eternal separation from Him.

4. The basis for choice is my own freedom. Man is his own plan of action. I am most a man when I make "authentic" choices, that is, choices which take into consideration the fact that "no man is an island unto himself" – what I do affects others – the effect of my choice on others must be taken into account by me.

   Buber and de Chardin would agree that I am free to make choices but my choices need to be based on an "informed conscience" that takes into account The Ten Commandments, the Pentateuch for Buber, and the Beatitudes for de Chardin. "Authentic Choices" for Buber and de Chardin are dependent on the basis for my choice, an "informed conscience" and on how my decision will affect others, not based solely on my opinion but also on the opinion(s) of the person(s) my choice will affect.

5. I , man, am "condemned to be free" – even though I did not create myself, I am responsible for all that follows once I exist. I am my own plan of action. To be free does not mean that I obtain what I wish for. It is rather the choice by which I decide to wish. Success in getting what I wish for is not important to freedom. Freedom is the ultimate reality – a value in itself. (Bernard J. Fleury, What is Man? pp.193-194)

   Buber and de Chardin would agree that we are "free" whether we like it or not, that we did not create ourselves, but are responsible for all that follows once I exist and have come to the age of reason.

   They would also agree with Sartre that freely making an authentic choice even though I don't get what I wished for is a good act. But they would not agree with him that my Freedom is the ultimate reality – a value in itself. God is the ultimate reality and choosing according to His perceived will for me is the proper moral exercise of my freedom to choose.

Article 9

Martin Buber's and Teilhard de Chardin's

View on Man Compared to B.F. Skinner's

Skinner believed that the basic "stuff" of the universe is physical matter, a substance which takes many forms.

Buber and de Chardin would absolutely disagree. The basic "stuff" of the universe is not "stuff" at all but a Being, The Light, Psychic Energy centered in One Divine Being, God, who is also a Person to Buber and Three Persons to deChardin, who is the source of all that is. Time begins when this Trinitarian God decides to share His life and the physical world, matter, the "without" of things, and the psychic world, spirit , consciousness, the "within" of things come into existence.

Skinner goes on to define Man as a biological organism who needs to be studied through a science of human behavior so that the behavior of man can be controlled and the human condition improved. It is human behavior that underlies the major problem of the human condition. The reason is our assumption that Man is a free-willing, free-thinking responsible entity. Autonomous Man has been assumed to be essentially mental and spiritual, free and responsible; a creator of thought, a source of action, an ultimate arbitrator of morality, value, and dignity. (Freedom and Dignity pp. 42-43, 58, 59, 81-82, 84, 88, 92, and 97) But to the contrary, Man is physical, not mental and spiritual; he is determined, not free and responsible; he is "created" by an environment which selects the actions of man by reinforcing them, thereby making them more likely to reoccur. Skinner's definition of Man and his assumption that the problem of controlling human behavior is the assumption of Autonomous Man lays the groundwork for his solution Behavior Modification through Operant Conditioning which he spells out in detail in Beyond Freedom and Dignity.

Buber and de Chardin's views are compatible with man being a biological organism in part but that is only the "without" of him, and omits the "within" which is the source of all the components that Skinner lists under Autonomous Man. To Buber and de Chardin these components are at the very core of what it means to be a man, to be human.

Skinner goes on to write that the technology of behavior eliminates only Autonomous Man. Man himself may be controlled by his environment but it is an environment which is almost wholly of is own making.

According to Skinner, Man's history and his genetic endowment are a far more reliable index to his behavior than his "will", his "spirit", or his "thought". In education and life this means that man learns to be what he is by the management and control of his interacting experience with the environment.

In a broad societal or world view this means control of predictable response to improve the human condition. Man is what man does; controlling man's doing improves man's being.

Buber and Sartre would agree that our environment shapes us and if it is so subtle that we do not even realize we are being programmed to believe or behave in a certain way, and so pervasive that we just get used to the control – like "everybody thinks or acts this way so it must be okay" we can indeed be controlled by such an environment – brainwashed into it.

They would also agree that Man's history in terms of what man does reveals a lot about human behavior. But behind man's overt behavior are his will, his thought, and his spirit – his moral compass.

Man is a biological organism but he is also a creature composed of body and soul and made in the image and likeness of God!

Bibliography

1. Brown, James M., Educational Implications of Four Conceptions of Human Nature. Washington , D.C.: The Catholic University of America Press, 1940. pp. xiii -139.
2. Buber, Martin, Between Man and Man. The Macmillan Company, New York, N.Y., 1972.
3. Buber, Martin, I and Thou. (Second Edition) Charles Schribner's Sons, New York, N.Y., 1958.
4. Culliton, Joseph T., A Processive World View for Pragmatic Christians. Philosophical Library, Inc., 5 East 40th St., New York, N.Y., 1975.
5. Dewey, John, Democracy and Education. New York: The MacMillan Company, 1925. pp. xii-434.
6. Dewey, John, Human Nature and Conduct. New York: Henry Holt and Company, 1915, pp, 134.
7. Fleury, Bernard J., A Comparative Study of the Philosophies of Education of John Dewey and Jacques Maritan: The University of Massachusetts, 1956. (an unpublished Master of Science Dissertation)

8. Fleury, Bernard J., <u>What is Man? Male and Female</u>. Bloomington, Indiana,
    AuthorHouse, 2011.
9. Sartre, Jean-Paul, <u>Being and Nothingness</u>. Washington Square Press, New York,
    N.Y., 1956.
10. Skinner, B. F., <u>Beyond Freedom and Dignity</u>: Alfred A. Knopf, New York, 1971.
11. Skinner, B. F., <u>Walden Two</u>. The Macmillan Co., New York, New York. 1948.
12. Teilhard de Chardin, Pierre, <u>The Phenomenon of Man</u>. New York: Harper and Row,
    Publishers, 1965.
13. Teilhard de Chardin, Pierre, <u>The Future of Man</u>. New York: Harper and Row,
    Publishers, 1969.
14. Teilhard de Chardin, Pierre, <u>Science and Christ</u>. New York: Harper and Row,
    Publishers. 1965.